"The poetry of Paul Krause exhibits clear and admirable characteristics. He knows that poetry, as an essential cultural activity, cannot be other than an activity of ethical significance. With this understanding, his verse exhibits two outstanding qualities. Being deeply conversant with the cultural foundations and traditions of the art, as evidenced in his essays, he appreciates the reach of language beyond the limits of much of the contemporary material and everyday world. His work thus transcends many of the usual current poetic concerns. Crucially, and now uncommonly in contemporary verse, he joins this understanding with translucent ethical sincerity. The combination of enriched language, transcendent concern, and personal sincerity distinguishes his voice and his verse. It is a poetry that deserves thoughtful readership."

Harold Jones, MA (Cantab),
New Zealand

"A classic wordsmith, Paul Krause crafts poetry that feels both fresh and eternal—full of warmth, wit, and wonder. This is a collection you will cherish for its lyricism, love, and thoughtful consideration on the human heart and soul."

Scott James Meyer
Professor of Practice
Sam Houston State University

I0805620

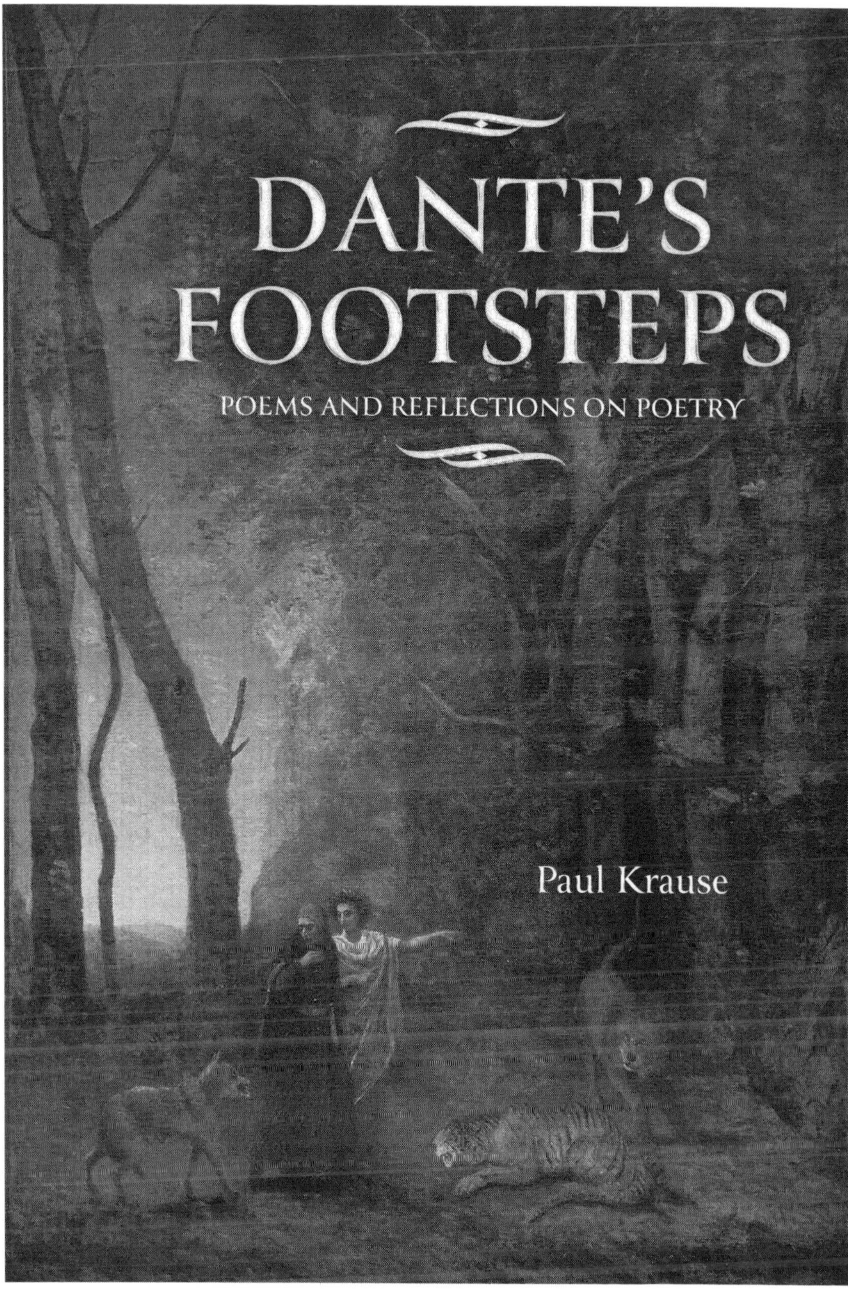

STONE TOWER PRESS

Dante's Footsteps

Stone Tower Press
7 Ellen Rd.
Middletown, RI 02842
stonetowerpress.com

Paperback ISBN: 979-8-9992313-1-4

Formatting and cover design by Amy Cole and Amy Landheer, JPL Design Solutions

Cover image: *Dante and Virgil* (Oil on canvas, 1859), Jean-Baptiste-Camille Corot
MFA Boston, image public domain

Printed in the United States of America

To Virgil, “sweet father” and “illustrious poet.”

TABLE OF CONTENTS

POEMS

ESSAYS AND REFLECTIONS

PREFACE

Poetry is at the heart of human nature and civilization. When one looks back over the history of civilization, it is often accompanied by, or begins with, poetry. The very apogee of the civilization in question inevitably converges with the age of poetic acme. Indeed, the very ascent of civilization and the spiritual vitality that accompanies civilization always stands alongside the poetry which inspired grand visions and the eloquence of language which the soul ascends to.

The rise of Hellenic civilization began not with Socrates, Plato, or Aristotle, but with Hesiod, Homer, and Sappho. What of the glory of Rome? Though not a poet, per se, Cicero's language stands unrivaled and makes him a spiritual poet, or a politician and philosopher of poetic verse one could say. Nevertheless, it is often to the poets Virgil, Ovid, Horace, and Statius where people point to when considering the grandeur of that city which once took the world captive. The "golden age" of Rome was preceded by the Golden Age of Latin literature, just as the golden age of Greece was preceded by the ingenuity of the Greek poets and playwrights.

Likewise, the rise of the splendor of English civilization is found in Chaucer, Spenser, Shakespeare, and Milton instead of Hobbes, Locke, or Mill. The revival of English high culture and civilization from the ruins of the late Enlightenment and Napoleonic Wars began with the explosion of romantic and Gothic literature and poetry by such names as Jane Austen, Lord Byron, and Charles Dickens, not to mention Wordsworth and Coleridge, among others. Their gifts are for the whole world and continue to move the soul long after their deaths.

Poetry is about love, the heavens, and the burning passion of the human heart that thirsts after Love itself. The Psalmist encapsulated the pulsating soul of poetry and the biblical drama long before the great poets of the Western tradition took to song: "O God, thou art my God; early will I seek thee: my soul thirsteth for thee, my flesh longeth for thee in a dry and thirsty land, where no water is; To see thy power and thy glory, so as I have seen thee in the sanctuary" (Psalm 63). Even upon the eve of the incarnation of Christ, the great flourishing of poetic biblical literature preceded it: Ecclesiastes, Song of Songs, Wisdom, and Sirach, as if to help announce to the world the coming of Love made flesh.

Consider, also, the formation of Germany and German culture. Though not yet a united political entity, the German Renaissance and the movement to a definitive German nation was preceded by the poetry of Novalis, Goethe, Hölderlin, and Schlegel.

The Russia of memory and consciousness, the Russia that is a gift to the world, was formed by torchbearers like Alexander Sumarokov, Vasily Zhukovsky, and Alexander Pushkin, who laid the groundwork for Dostoevsky and Tolstoy and their gifts to the world which inspired Pasternak and Solzhenitsyn. Literature, but especially poetry, can foster spiritual birth or resuscitation as is the universal case seen throughout history.

Before the rise of Christianity, the Mediterranean world moved with a flurry of love poetry which prepared it for Christianity: Homer, Virgil, Ovid, Horace, and Statius. The project of the Roman literati, even those outside of poetry, was to rekindle the spirit of *pietas*—what we call piety, which had been lost in the decadence of the republic and the civil wars and paved the way for the Gospel in Roman lands. The spiritual heights of the high Middle Ages and Renaissance were preceded by *Beowulf*, *The Song of Roland*, *The Poem of the Cid*, the Troubadours, and, of course, Dante and *The Divine Comedy*.

Humans are language animals; this is why poetry has always had the power to move the very core of humans from its inception to today. As Dante so brilliantly wrote, "Here let death's poetry arise to life, O Muses sacrosanct whose liege I am! And let Calliope rise up and play her sweet accompaniment in the same strain that pierced the wretched magpies with the truth of unforgivable presumptuousness." But every culture, every civilization, and every great monument that enchants the soul has love at its heart and can move the heart to the Good, True, and Beautiful.

The eternality of permanent things, from buildings to literature to the very lives of the saints, is rooted in their dedication to Love. For it was Love that Dante abandoned that led him to the "dark wilderness" and Love which set him back on "the straight and true" and prepped him "to climb unto the stars." And it has long been the desire for Love that has moved the poets to capture the universal yearning of the human heart. Throughout *The Divine Comedy*, Dante asserts that poetry—properly and purely understood—directs us to God.

Language that does not have love pulsating through its heart is a language that dissipates and is forgotten. The unforgettable words of Genesis, "In the beginning, God created the heavens and the earth," are immortal because those words were spoken from the mouth of Love itself. The great works of literature, even from those of now dead languages, poetically live on because of the love which moved those words to the heavens. As such, they shall never die because they are the words that imitate the Word who is Love itself. It is precisely for this reason why Dante can be directed to the stars of Heaven by the poets of love which reveal to us, though in imperfect ways, glimpses of the beauty and love of God.

If there is a spiritual resurrection, which is the true cure for the ailments of modernity and our current civilizational malaise, it will be accompanied and preceded by a linguistic and literary resurrection.

This has been the pattern of history. This is the timeless and eternal truth that undergirds human nature itself.

Poetry and language awaken the soul because the true essence of poetry and language is love. God created through a poetic spoken word. As Johann Hamann said, "poetry is the mother tongue of humans." And the tongue which thirsts after Love can only be satisfied by drinking from the well of Love itself. Throughout history, we find that a poetic civilization aimed at Love flourishes; it is our task as Christians to reclaim this profound truth about poetry and civilization for the future of our culture and civilization. We might also find that it is a catalyst for a new spiritual revitalization as well.

POEMS

I

NATURE

AS THE LEAVES BEGIN TO CHANGE

As the leaves begin to change
You see my soul start to play
Atop that misty mountain
Gazing out across the bay.

With winds howling at my back
And leaves tumbling in the breeze,
With birds singing in my ears,
And the setting sun, I'm free.

As the leaves begin to change
The world calls us far away
Green grass, red trees, and orange skies
All moving to Beauty's sway.

In that waltz, you find me now
Singing, dancing, with the moon
While my soul climbs up on high
Always dreaming about you.

DANCE OF THE SKY

As I look up at the stars
That sing to me from afar,
I dwell in that spirit divine
Giving life to this soul of mine.

My eyes gazing on the moon,
Whose dance shall end very soon,
Will rest to shining silver
But rise to golden splendor.

WHERE THE WILD FLOWERS GROW

Where the wildflowers grow
My feet are light and silent
Beneath the fireflies' bright glow.

Where the wildflowers grow
I lay next to giants
Holding hands enjoying the show.

Where the wildflowers grow
I gaze upon the bumblebees
Listening to the river flow.

Where the wildflowers grow
I rest where none can see
The newborn fawn and mother doe.

Where the wildflowers grow
Birds sing songs from tall groves
Despite the rain, sleet, and snow.

Now a shovel digs deep below
To find my body and bones
Where the wildflowers grow.

A WALK IN THE WOODS

Over that orange wall of leaves
Where spirits and wind roam free,
The fluttering butterflies, fireflies,
And sprouted daisies soar on high
Under that sunny pink mist of haze,
Singing and dancing at the end of day.

As my legs and feet do tread,
Becoming like a tumbling leaf
Twisting over endless fields
Drifting higher and higher,
Climbing closer and closer,
To where my soul finds concord.

WALKING IN THE NIGHT

The moon dances across the black sky
With the stars shining bright for me tonight.
The whispering winds are telling me their healing secrets
As the choir of crickets softly sing their sweet lullabies.
So now I tread through the dark of night with new life
As the trees smile and wave to me goodnight.
The moon's gaze pulls me in tight,
Awakening my soul from those drowsy steps,
Guiding me home and making me one
With the song and waltz of that nighttime bliss.

WINTER'S ROAR

In that harsh sea of endless white,
With whipping winds hungry to bite,
Roars a lonely howl, far out of sight.

SUNRISE

The sun rises in the sky
And awakens my eyes to that sight
So beautiful: the light chasing
Away the mist, formed from the night.

THE HIKE

On country roads
And rocky steps
My legs do tread,
That hallowed ground
Of mountains old.

As I walk on high
The birds are singing
The squirrels are eating
The trees are clapping
The wind is dancing.

Souls, far and wide have come
To answer Nature's call
Where all hearts become one
Beating, beating, beating
To the setting of the sun.

NATURE'S INVITATION

At the lake
In the hills
My eyes see
And ears hear

The dance of the nymphs
The song of the wind
And hands of the leaves
Reaching out to me.

MORNING DEW

Cover me in morning dew
To wake and see only you
Softly sleeping and dreaming,
A soul splendidly beaming.

II

BALLADS

LYING ON MOONLIT SAND

Lying on moonlit sand, there
We wept as I held him tight.
"Kiss me, kiss me, my love, and
Set me free this very night."

Lying on moonlit sand, his
Eyes fading like waning seas
"Forgive me, and bless me my love,
Too long I waited for thee."

Lying on moonlit sand, the
Storm roaring infernally;
So I kissed him in my arms,
Then ash rose eternally.

ONE WITH THE SEA

The waves rock and roil over the turbulent sea
Calling my soul to that forbidden horizon
Where my ears can listen to those songs and be made free.

Beneath that white foam and whispering water, sings a siren
Gently pulling me close to her
To gaze into those eyes that cause my heart to stir.

My heart now rocks and roils inside of me,
With her voice singing to my soul: leap and be free!
So I shackle chains upon my feet to become one with the sea.

THE BALLAD OF MARGARUITE AND SIR GODFREY

I wait for thee at night,
My gallant and handsome knight,
To gallop back home to me
Whose face I long to see.

Beneath death's dark tomb where shadows sleep,
For thee my severed head does weep,
A knight once powerful and bold,
Whose deadly demise shall never be told.

At the rising of the sun
My burning heart sinks deep,
And my sickening soul does weep:
When shall you return to me, my Love, so you and I can become one?

Beneath the ground my heart still beats
To reunite with my Love so sweet.
Death's culling blow did not defeat
My love for you, oh sweet Margaruite!

By noonday's tide, a horse does stride
Without its knight so valiant and true
Which causes my eyes to cry:
Godfrey, Godfrey, have you died too?

Up from death's dark tomb where shadows sleep
My hands and arms fight to break free,
To rise from this grave so dark and deep
And ride to you, my Love, whose eyes I yearn to see.

Your armor, dear Godfrey, is now a tapestry of dreams.
Beneath the rising moon I do cry and sing
For your phantom to come and set me free:
Return to me, my Love, and be thou my king!

Do not weep for me, my Love so sweet,
For you I rode to accomplish my feats.
On Judgement Day, when the trumpet once again sings,
We shall soar to heaven on an eagle's wings.

Out in the forest, dark, a voice does call to me.
I pray that it is you, my Love, singing in that handsome key.
A risen knight in the night, to hold me as I cry,
With love forever burning in your heart, and stars shining in
your eyes.

THE KISS

On that lonely mountaintop
Looking out across the bay
Dance the birds, fish, and nereids
As blue, white, waves crash and sway

On the rocks I climb and dive
List'ning softly to her songs.
Her hair, her eyes, and her face
My soul and heart fully longs.

On that lonely mountaintop
Looking out across the bay
"Kiss me, Kiss me, my love, and
Let us sing and dance today."

On that golden sand we dance
In each other's arms and gaze,
Until dust and ash we turn
Beneath Love's last shining ray.

HENRY'S PRAYER (OR MY DEAR HENRY)

Remember me, O Eleanor,
My Love so sweet and pure.
For you I fought, so our
Love could last and endure.

Where are you, my dear Henry,
Whose eyes I weep to see,
Wanting to rest my cheek upon your cheek,
Singing songs so pure and free.

In the muck and mud I rest,
Dreaming of our love forever blessed.
As I close my eyes, to you I cry:
Pray for me, my Dear, for now I die.

The sun fades in the darkening sky
As my heart and soul sink with terrible sighs:
Is that you, my dear Henry,
Riding down the road I spy?

WHERE THE NEREIDS SWIM AND PLAY

Where the Nereids swim and play
On golden sand there I lay
Under the sun, moon, and stars
My heart does look from afar.

Where the Nereids swim and play
On ship and sea I now stay
In the heat of summer's June
And beneath the pale white moon.

Where the Nereids swim and play
I hear them sing as I lay
To cast my net and my heart
'Till no more I feel apart.

Where the Nereids swim and play
I sing and dance in the bay.
Now at last, that hour comes
I sink with the setting sun.

III

CULTURE

THE SONG OF AENEAS

O holy city destroyed by Greece's sons
My sighs did cry and rise from my lungs.
Ah me! I beg of thee, Muse, to come
And sing sweet songs until I see the sun.
This bleeding pain that tears away my heart,
Rips all my body, mind, and soul apart.
Those ravenous howls hissing through my ears
As I walk alone bringing me to tears,
Shrieking screams of infants piercing my soul
Lest you save me with a song that consoles.

Step by step on those sandy dunes I did tread,
Where all my family and friends once bled
In flashing helmets, armed with sword and spear
I trembled with the earth as he drew near.
Those eyes gleaming red with fiery blood
Came rushing at us like a crashing flood.
One swing of his arm and our life was done
Gods and men all broke and turned to run.
Back to my native home I wept and fled
Feet fleeing fast as I was filled with dread.

Nothing now left but the winds and sands of time,
So I fell on my knees knowing my crime.
Last of the noble Trojan race I cried
Thinking it so much better to have died.
By Heaven! that splendid light I did see
And quickly blinded as you came to me.
What gallant songs you whispered in my ears
That sweetly swept aside all of my fears.

Shouts of "Aeneas" sounding through the air
His tale you told me to sing and to share.

At first I did not know that song of sorrow
That began, "Arma virumque cano."
Unconscious of eternal future fame
I wandered and blabbered words without shame
Filled with a happiness that consumed me,
As your words renewed my heart to be free.
Though war be a harsh mistress, Jove still lives
With those sweet songs that always give and give.
Soon, soon, shall the conquest be completed
When the proud are subdued and defeated.

THE MYRMIDON

Long ago and far away
Over stormy seas and plains
To fight for that famous girl
Known across the whole, wide, world.

Flashing helmets and roaring waves
Crashed and thundered o'er the plains.
For glory, honor, and freedom, yet we were but slaves
As gods and kings turned us into prey.

"For Troy!" he said.
"For Honor!" he said.
"For Helen!" he said.
On the beaches of Troy, we bled.

"Forward to the walls!" he said.
On the sands of Troy, we bled.
"Charge for the walls!" he said.
On the walls of Troy, we bled.

"Honor my name," I said.
"I will, my friend."
"Don't forget me," I said.
"Your story I shall tell my son in bed."

Long ago and far away
Over stormy seas and plains
A body discovered, burned infernally,
But whose name now echoes through eternity.

TO VIRGIL

For Hannah Taylor

Oh how I weep to read
That Mantuan poet much older than me
Whose words are filled with beauty and grace
Bringing tears and smiles to my face.

A KNIGHT'S QUEST

In ruins filled with death and darkness
A knight in shining armor strode
To undo this dying world's cruel harshness
And claim the sword lost in the Lake of Shadows.

The night was calm and the moon shone pale,
With the castle on the hill calling to him: come and find the grail.
So the knight rode on, his steed steady, both unready to fail:
Onward, onward, so others may tell our tale.

DANTE AND OVID

I read he who sings of snakes
And marble turning into
Humans. Endless change and
Turbulence consuming all,
Causing our soaring ascent
To crash, burn, and sadly fall.

Next I read he who cries for
The fallen, weeping graceful
Tears beside broken souls in
Need of heavenly loving.
Be silent, Ovid, and join
The chorus, where love orders
All things and does restore us.

CAMPALDINO

Do not say this is a sad goodbye,
Though to a horse and arms I fly,
To sally forth with lance and shield ready to die.

Not a day goes by I do not think of thee,
When your eyes on that bridge did call to me,
Though my heart in cowardice raced to flee.

I hope you think of me, wherever you are,
And do not feel any wounds or scars,
But instead look on high toward the shining stars.

Now the trumpet calls,
So I must stand tall,
To fight for your love, of which I'm ready to fall.

DANTE'S FOOTSTEPS

I met a pilgrim as if by fate
While so far from Beauty's grace.
Two shadows crossed on the sand
But I, face down, saw but land.

My heavy painful days never end
Trapped in darkness without friends,
Underneath rock and thunder,
Wailing screams without wonder.

Love ripped from my heart due to pride,
Heavenly steps crossed my side.
Theirs the walk of Love's duty
Bringing forth light and beauty.

Echoes now of those footsteps weary
Climbing towards Mother Mary.
But I'm stuck in transgression
Eternally cut off from heaven.

FRANCESCA'S LAMENT

A man came to me at night
And consoled me in my flight.
He looking upward at me,
I looking downward on he.

Whipped about in twists and turns
My heart does forever burn.
But in that tiny moment
His sweet voice of atonement

Sung care for me and Paolo.
So I wept to him our woe;
He cried tears of compassion
For our idolatrous sin.

But my heart cannot have rest,
That sweet voice faded and left.
Love disappeared in thin air,
Heaven sings joy; I, despair.

IV

METAPHYSICAL

WHEN TIME WALKED WITH ME

Farewell, O Beautiful Time
Now that thou hath let go of my hand,
And sang that mystic chord so fine
Till my soul came to rest and died.
From babbling sounds
To pulling crawl on the ground,
You lifted me up as I stood and fell upon my face,
And stretched forth my legs to run my sacred race.

You were with me when my grieving soul did fly,
Fleeing from that broken earthly grossness
Across that valley of weeping tears and shattered brokenness
Eyes tormented, body dented, and soul repented.
Until those clouds overhead gave way
And the light of heaven shined forth from across the bay,
Calling me home to that Beauty long hidden
Which my sight at long last humbly accepted.

You, O Time, graceful and never failing,
Departed from me with a blissful kiss,
My soul no more enslaved to the burning cauldron's hiss
Soared to that promised joy and love which consumed me,
And brought me, like a flood, unto the beatitudes of Eternity.

THE FALL OF ADAM

From Eden's bed of red roses these hands did gather
Flowers from the Garden beneath eternity's lustrous azure,
A crown of choicest flowers to welcome the return of fair Eve
But then I saw her weeping beneath that forbidden tree.

With eyes of water, proof of her repentant heart
I walked to her with my soul torn apart.
That crown of flowers turned to ash in my hands
And dissolved to dust as it dropped onto land.

Yet I could not live without my wife so dear,
So I wept in her arms, cries of regret but not of fear,
Pleading with those tears to rise up to heaven
The truest expression of my guilty confession.

ON LOOKING AT THE FALL OF MILTON'S ADAM AND EVE

In the twilight of Eden's bloom
Where the Sun of God kisses the trees,
A rapturous world of delight once did swoon
Adam and Eve, our first parents, into love's perfect harmony.

With eyes of envy the Devil gazed
Through fog, mist, and haze
Looking upon our first father and matron mother
Tormented without his other.

O to hell with them I say!
As I grieve and grieve, cut off from Love's eternal way
Forever lost in my own passions pining since that day
I fell from heaven's blessèd ray.

Look at them, in each other's arms and sway
Light of the light of this world!
No more, no way!
They shall descend with me into darkness where their cries will
be unheard
Caught in death's despondent day.

With eyes innocent and pure
Adam to Eve spoke he:
Light of this world, and heaven's holiest allure:
Be thou my queen, and take this crown I made for thee.

To whom Eve thus did cry:
Adam, sweetest husband so pure and kind,
Look upon this fruit I did spy
Tempted to eat, and did, and now shall surely die.

Then did the Serpent laugh, as that cruel hiss and hollow sound
Through Eden resounded in supposèd triumph of their
bliss unbound.
Their tears dropping and mingling with earth's weeping woe,
despoiled on the spot
As shame, and guilt, and envy caused the world to furl and rot.

From that heavenly voice our parents wept and ran,
Until, with one last look, Adam to Eve thus began:
Let us trust in God who is never unkind,
That if into your breasts and arms I fly
With kisses no longer pure, but love still evermore,
We may be cleansed from sin with God's love and grace that
will surely win this eternal war.
And though dust we are and to dust we shall return
Until the Victor takes captivity captive and from the grave,
hand in hand we turn
With eyes set once more to heaven
And be ushered, new body and soul, into the eternal procession.

THE SWAN SONG OF MILTON'S ADAM

Oh that blissful beauty brought forth by Love,
Luminous light of life, apple of my eye,
Of which I dream at night. Depart from me not.
Mend my mortal heart to thy fire so hot.
Let me forever see, thy lustrous pastures green,
Filled with honeybees and stars glist'ning sheen.
Where birds in choirs sing, about thy grace,
Drawing me nearer to thee, to see thy eternal face.
So now I sing and dance, with that woman so blest
Whom thou did not create by chance,
Thus hand in hand we go, to your transcendent home,
To live, laugh, and love, in thy eternal rest.

THE COMING OF THE SON OF LOVE

From the heavens descend
The Son of Love eternally sent
To heal our hearts and soul
So we may be made forever whole.

THE NIGHT OF CHRIST'S NATIVITY

The sky sings to me tonight
And guides my eyes to that star so bright
Where shepherds walk upon sand and plain
With sheep and lamb by their side,
Walking with gentle strides,
Knowing that the world is blessed
And no creature shall be slain,
And soon they may have a blessèd rest.

The wind whistles with a thoughtful prayer
As I tread on sand and stone,
When thus, a gentle spirit appears in the air:
"A new king is born to claim the throne,
Seek him not with a golden crown or sword
Though he is your lord to sing and adore.
That star you see which captures your gaze
You will follow for nights and days
Till you find, in a mountain cave,
The newborn king who will become a slave
And save the world and your soul
Whom you and the nations shall extol."

ESSAYS AND REFLECTIONS

HOMER'S EPIC OF LOVE

"Rage—Goddess, sing the rage of Peleus' son Achilles." When we think of Homer's *Iliad* we immediately think of war. Images of the greatest warrior, Achilles, often soar into our mind; but so too do other warriors like Prince Hector. Blood, carnage, and death are what we generally associate with the epic. We may even erroneously think it as the Greek equivalent of the Bible with stories of Alexander the Great sleeping with it during his conquest of Persia. *The Iliad*, however, isn't a work that celebrates the horror of war but unmasks and deconstructs it. Over the course of this undressing of the naked brutality of war and the capriciousness of the gods, Homer asserts humanistic love is the most heroic reality of human life and existence which includes, most importantly, love of enemies.

Achilles is the hero of the *Iliad*; this we all know. The epic opens in song to Achilles, the goddesses, gods, and muses singing of Achilles and his warlike wrath that decimated Troy. That the song centers on Achilles is important. Though a demigod, his association with the wrath of the divines is revealed using the word *mēnis* (a word exclusively used for the rage of the gods and not of men). Achilles, therefore, is introduced as something divine-like, but his "divinity" is tied to rage, wrath, death, destruction.

Yet Achilles is a man, therefore mortal, and also a lover. For love is only something experienced and shown in the human world in Homer's great epic. This, too, is something the reader must be aware of. All the instances of wondrous love that warm our heart and cause us to remember the landscape of the *Iliad*, are instances of love manifested by humans and only humans. The gods cannot love. Only humans can. That is a subtle, indeed radical, statement by our poet. And that journey to humanization in love, especially as it relates to Achilles, is what the *Iliad* is ultimately about.

It is impossible to understand Homer without Hesiod. The two greatest poets of the ancient Greek tradition couldn't be more different. Hesiod's *Theogony* sings the praises of gods and wars, violence and lust. Homer sings of men and their love. The gods may both be bloodthirsty and lusty in Hesiod and Homer, but Homer isn't concerned with giving the gods their due piety or praise as Hesiod is. Moreover, their understanding of the cosmos radically differ: Hesiod's cosmos is moved by lust and violence; Homer's cosmos, though constrained by the dictates of the gods, opens up with the possibility of healing redemption and peace through human agency. Hesiod's poem is a celebration of the sublime, dark, and grisly violence of the divines. Homer's epic is a deconstruction of the Hesiodic fantasy and a subtle proclamation of the power of human love and agency despite all the forces of death, destruction, and darkness that is arrayed against it.

Additionally, Homer invents a word that the lands once saturated by the Christian religion know: *agape*. Homer has the first written use of the word (he uses multiple variations of it, but the root agape is there) and it denotes affection for the dead, a love for the deceased or injured—in other words, a self-giving kindness to a beloved. The Septuagint translators, seeking to find a Greek word that expressed such compassion they associated with the love of Adonai, borrowed from Homer and brought it into its now elevated, biblical, and eventually Christian (thanks to the New Testament writers quoting from the Septuagint). For Homer's use of the term came closest to expressing a love rooted in compassion to others.

Achilles's metamorphosis from divine, inhuman, killer to loving human, the man whose act of *agape* toward Priam brings the epic to its incredible conclusion, is what Homer is singing about. This should be obvious when we do encounter the war scenes throughout the epic—even without Achilles present in the fighting that dominates much of the poem. When men die, Homer's often bloody and captivating description of arms and necks being hacked and blood pouring out of bowels is subtly offset by the tender humanization of the dead. The men who die, Homer also describes, are husbands, fathers, and sons. For example, in describing the death of Simoisius: "And Telamonian Ajax struck Anthemion's son, the hardy stripling Simoisius, still unwed. His mother had borne him along the Simois' banks when she trailed her parents down the slopes of Ida to tend their flocks, and so they called him Simoisius. But never would he repay his loving parents now for the gift of rearing—his life cut short so soon." Homer reminds us that the deceased are the same as you and I.

The evolution of the love which Homer sings can bring healing in the world is associated with three principal characters (four if we count Priam). There is the filial love of Hector (and Priam). Then there is the compassion and merciful love, the "kindness," of Patroclus. Then there is the final manifestation of love by Achilles to his avowed enemy—Priam. The love we witness is also chronological insofar that the touching scenes of the love which bring momentary respites of peace and healing is first revealed by Hector, then by Patroclus, and reaching its magnanimous achievement in Achilles.

That Hector is a man of filial piety is not lost to any reader of the epic. When Hector's brother, Helenus, persuades Hector to safely return to Troy, he also reminds him of the duty to offer up libations to Athena's shrine which the pious prince of Troy does. Inside of Troy, after battle, Hector instructs the women of the city to "Pray to the gods." Homer also describes Hector's heart as "rac[ing] to help [his] Trojans."

But the most tender and memorable moment of Hector's filial love comes when he stands on the battlements of the city. War and destruction wage over the city walls. Hector is fully dressed in military garb. His infant son, Astyanax, cowers in fear from the sight of this shadowy and vicious warrior. In a loving moment, Hector disarms and disrobes himself revealing himself with a human face and caressing hands as he cradles his son and ends the babe's weeping. In the presence of his family, this act of filial love brings momentary peace, a brief moment of serenity to the story even though we all know Hector's fate. But in this moment, love and peace have triumphed.

Touching though this filial love is, Homer is also going further: filial love is not enough to bring peace to a war-torn world. Hector, as we know, eventually passes Astyanax to Andromache, rearms himself, and ventures out into the chaotic world of death and destruction to continue the war. Yet this human moment has often been memorialized in painting down through the ages and is a manifestation of the power of the love that binds families together in the face of hardship and destruction. Consider it. The world around Hector, Andromache, and Astyanax is crumbling. War is consuming their city. It will consume their city. In the midst of that death and destruction that envelopes them their love brings a brief respite, a beautiful pause, a peace that foreshadows where Homer is taking the epic.

If filial love is not enough, the love that Homer praises but goes beyond evolves into kindness to the wounded, the injured, the maimed. This is the love that moves the heart of Patroclus, "the best of the Greeks." Contrary to most media depictions, Patroclus was not younger than Achilles. He was the elder individual in the friendship the two shared. As an older sage, Patroclus is also a healer. He is healer of wounded women (Briseis) and wounded men (Eurypylus). The love that Homer attaches to Patroclus is one of kindness and compassion, a kindness and compassion that brings healing into the wounded world.

As the Greeks are retreating to their ships, a severely injured Eurypylus staggers into camp with an arrow wound. Patroclus recognizes his comrade and immediately tends his grave wounds. Without Patroclus's intervention, Eurypylus would have died.

It could have been easy for Patroclus to remain indifferent to the suffering of his comrades (as Achilles was at the time). Instead, in an act of his own volition, Patroclus defies Achilles's command not to aid the rest of the Greeks until Agamemnon humbles himself and begs Achilles's forgiveness for his affront of taking Briseis. Patroclus, in tender mercy and kindness toward his wounded brethren, rushes to Eurypylus's aid:

> "And bracing the captain, arm around his waist, he helped him toward his shelter. An aide saw them and put some oxhides down. Patroclus stretched him out, knelt with a knife and cut the sharp, stabbing arrow out of Eurypylus' thigh and washed the wound clean of the dark running blood with clear warm water. Pounding it in his palms, he crushed a bitter root and covered over the gash to kill his comrade's pain, a cure that fought off every kind of pain...and the wound dried and the flowing blood stopped."

Here is yet another beautiful moment of respite, healing in the midst of death, that Homer gives us. Patroclus cares for Eurypylus's wound. Patroclus heals Eurypylus of his injury and pain. The actions of Patroclus save the Greek captain. Patroclus has literally brought healing into this bleak world of death and destruction.

This loving kindness, moved by the spirit of mercy toward others, goes beyond the filial love we have previously witnessed with Hector. Though Patroclus eventually joins battle to help the Greeks as the Trojans are bearing down on the beachhead threatening to destroy the ships that are needed to take the soldiers back home and dies by Hector's hand, the struggle to reclaim Patroclus's body reveals an even greater spirit of kindness from the soul of Patroclus. After the Greeks recover the body of Patroclus and return it to Achilles, Briseis arrives and offers a great lament that further reveals Patroclus's kind and loving soul:

> "But you, Patroclus, you would not let me weep, not when the swift Achilles cut my husband down, not when he plundered the lordly Mynes' city—not even weep! No, again and again you vowed you'd make me godlike Achilles' lawful, wedded wife, you would sail me west in your warships, home to Phthia and there with the Myrmidons hold my marriage feast. So now I mourn your death—I will never stop—you were always kind."

Kindness.

Through Patroclus, Homer is slowly evolving and revealing the heroic power of love. The love of Patroclus is one step closer to the love that will bring peace and healing to the cosmos. Patroclus was "kind to all," as Menelaus said in remembering Patroclus as he fought to recover his slain body. Patroclus's kindness was mostly shown to his comrades, his friends, but as revealed by Briseis, also to a wounded enemy (her). That kindness to others, including an outsider, an avowed enemy, is the love that Achilles will now embody from his friend and elevate into a new cosmic dimension in dealing with Priam. Kindness, as revealed in the life of Patroclus—his true heroism—extends not only to fellow braves and countrymen but also to outsiders, enemies who are also wounded and aggrieved by the horror of war (as Briseis was).

The death of Patroclus, as we know, inflames the rage of Achilles. He goes on a killing spree. He fights gods and men alike. He slays the innocent and defenseless Lycaon. He kills Trojan soldiers left and right as he cuts a path to Hector. Then he slays Hector and attempts to defile Hector's body and returns to his tent.

In this sequence of events, the inhumanity of Achilles is manifested for us to see. Defenseless Lycaon throws himself, naked and unarmed, at the feet of Achilles begging for his life. Achilles rebuffs his foe, "Drawing his sharp sword Achilles struck [Lycaon's] collarbone just beside the neck and the two-edged blade drove home, plunging to the hilt—and down on the ground he sprawled, stretched facefirst and dark blood pouring out of him drenched the earth. Achilles grabbed a foot, slung him into the river, washed away downstream as he cried above him savage words to wing him on his way." In fighting the Scamander River and slaying men all over the battlefield, the rage of Achilles is everything wrong with the cosmos. Harshness. Cruelty. Death. Destruction. Hector initially tries to reason with Achilles but loses his nerve when he sees the ravenous eyes of Achilles. Achilles then slays Hector with the help of Athena (furthering Homer's association of the gods with a bleak cruelty).

We return to question of filial love when Priam ventures into the tent of Achilles. Achilles, in his rage, had vowed to wipe out the seed of Priam from the face of the earth. To vanish his avowed foe, to bring destruction to those who have harmed him and his soul.

Repeating the image of cruelty we have just witnessed with Lycaon throwing himself defenselessly at the feet of Achilles, Priam throws himself at the feet of Achilles and weeps for mercy and the return of Hector's body. Here, if imagery is meant to repeat itself, Achilles should have slaughtered his enemy. Instead, Priam's love for Hector and the filial love that gave him the courage to venture into enemy territory and enter the tent of the murderous Achilles unarmed breaks the capricious heart of Achilles. Achilles's memory is rekindled with the love of his father, Peleus. He lifts up Priam, not as an enemy, but as a friend. He embraces him in love rather than animosity.

We have also witnessed this image of embrace in a dialectic of contrasts. There has been the embrace of cruelty and death. There has also been the embrace of compassion and love. Routinely throughout the battle scenes, embrace has been accompanied by death. The two most famous being Achilles with Lycaon and Hector. Then there were the images of embrace reflecting love: Hector and his family; Patroclus and Eurypylus; Briseis and Patroclus; now Achilles and Priam.

This embrace of Priam marks the humanization of Achilles, the culmination of his metamorphosis from the cosmic callousness of the gods which he has so far been associated with to the human love of tenderness, mercy, and kindness exhibited by the likes of Hector, Patroclus, Briseis, and Priam. Achilles has a human moment. And in that human moment he finds his freedom—freed from the divine rage that has enslaved him.

Without compulsion from the gods or Agamemnon, Achilles's embrace of Priam in love leads the captain of the myrmidons to not only return the body of Hector for a proper funeral but also to bestow a temporary peace to his enemy in order to give Hector the proper affection due to him. Achilles's action not only reflects a love to Priam, but it also reflects a newfound love—respect and understanding—for Hector. Achilles's act of forgiveness liberates him from his own constraints. Forgiveness, here, isn't about forgetting. It is about the freedom to live a new life and to chart a new path for the self despite all that has happened—to embrace a new active spirit in the face of all the adversities that this life throws against us. This is what Achilles achieves at the conclusion of the *Iliad* and this is what Homer is proclaiming as the most heroic thing any of us can achieve. Centuries later, Aristotle would remark that the kindness shown to an enemy, an outsider, is an embodiment of all that is beautiful and noble. That Homer achieves this in his poetic masterpiece is a testament to his forward thinking and ethical rhetoric.

Homer knew the rest of the story as we do. But that's not the story Homer gave to posterity. Instead, the *Iliad* ends with peace. A peace that explicitly proclaims that only love—a love directed to our enemies rooted in forgiveness of the rage and animosity—can bring healing into the world. The heroism that Homer sings of is not war but love, and it is the exclusive domain of us mortals which makes it so precious. No Trojan horse. No sack and burning of Troy. No death of Achilles. This is not accidental on Homer's part; to end the story on Achilles's embrace of Priam and his bestowing peace to the grieving king is the message that the epic has been working to. Although the

Iliad sings of the rage turned to love of Achilles, the last name sung of in the poem is the enemy of the Greeks, the valiant foe of Achilles, the son of Priam: "Hector, tamer of horses."

From an intertextual perspective, especially in the concentration of the imagery and the language employed by Homer, the *Iliad* isn't celebrating gory and destructive violence as simplistic readings would have one believe. On the contrary, Homer deconstructed the destructive violent fantasy of Hesiod and the pre-Homeric poetic tradition and offered a humanized reading of Greek mythic consciousness which advanced our own humanist sensibilities which have reverberated down through the ages. Homer's *Iliad* is nothing short of a monumental achievement in ushering in a new human consciousness of what matters in life: love of family, kindness to others, forgiveness to enemies.

As we know from the Greek context, memory is what lives on forever. Memory is what we have and bestow. Homer took the memory of the Trojan War, its story and heroes, and subverted its violence and tragedy to create a new memory rooted in love, a love that extends to enemies and brings about peace. In a stroke of what we would consider modern genius, Homer understood the power of narrative and offered a new narrative that would humanize us and make us more compassionate.

Homer inverts the world he knew from Hesiod and the story that his compatriots knew well. That world of dark gods and cruel violence that characterizes Hesiod's cosmos is still part of Homer's cosmos, to be sure, but Homer opens the cosmos to human agency, an agency principally tied to love that is absent the nature of the gods but is the heroic part of human nature. For the gods cannot, and do not, love in Homer's epic. Only humans love. Homer's *Iliad* is, in fact, a love story of epic, cosmic, proportions. It ends on a note of peace brought forth by an act of forgiveness and embrace of an enemy. It captures the totality of the human condition: rage, wrath, war, death, destruction but also romance, passion, love, mercy, forgiveness, and hope. That is why it stands unrivaled in the history of human literature and will continue to be read for all eternity.

VIRGIL AND THE CHRISTIAN IMAGINATION

"Love conquers all things; let us yield to love." It would be perfectly reasonable to misattribute this quote to a famous early church father or a book from the Bible. Instead, it is from the great Roman poet Virgil.

Anyone familiar with Dante's *Divine Comedy* will remember that Virgil is a prominent character, serving as Dante's guide through hell and purgatory. Saint Augustine, while critical of aspects of Virgil's mythopoetic political theology, held him in great esteem and went so far as to call him the "best and most renowned of all poets." Furthermore, T. S. Eliot considered Virgil the greatest poet of the Western tradition and called the *Aeneid* "our classic."

Why was Virgil so important to generations in the past, and why does he remain an indispensable figure for our adrift lives today? In *De Doctrina Christiana*, Augustine provided a lengthy commentary on the relationship between signs and things. The beauty of things in the world, Augustine wrote, is ultimately and properly a sign of the beauty and truth that emanates from the uniquely beautiful and truthful thing: God Himself. In the *Confessions* and in his rebukes to the Manicheans on Genesis, Augustine also remarked that all of material creation has some level of beauty to it since it subsists in God's loving wisdom, even if we can't quite see or understand the beauty, for instance, of a fly or maggot.

One of the most common Virgilian themes aligns with this theological conviction: love is the most powerful force in the world. The power of love is all consuming and all desiring, and Virgil's advice is to give oneself over to the desire and power of love. Many later Christians came to recognize the basic truth to Virgil's poetic proclamations of how yielding to love can transform the soul.

In the *Eclogues* Gallus is a dying, lovesick, man who yearns to be consumed by love—a love which he himself knows well but could not consummate in life. In the serenity of his countryside estate, the Elysian idyll if there ever was one, he utters those immortal words: *Omnia vincit amor: et nos cedamus amori*. Love conquers all; let us yield to love!

Of course, Gallus says this tragically. As we know, he loved Lycoris and devoted himself to her. She, however, didn't reciprocate and eventually abandoned him. Thus, Gallus wallows alone in isolation and grows "mad" with his memories of love and desire for love. Even the gods were unable to cure Gallus from his spell of love signifying how love stands above the pagan deities, love transcends all material things.

The failure of the gods to break the spell of love reveals Virgil's insight that love is the greatest and grandest thing in the cosmos, for it is beyond even the control of the gods. In suffering or in joy, we cannot escape the consuming power of the fire of love itself. If only Lycoris had yielded to love the two would have been together in tender intimacy until their dying breaths. This, it seems, is what Virgil is subtly promoting: for love to conquer, two creatures must yield to its invitation.

Benedict XVI reminded Christians in Deus Caritas Est that God is a God of both eros and agape. God is a burning and devouring flame of love that desires all humans to experience love, beauty, and happiness. Being made in the image of God (*imago Dei*) means all humans also exude that flame of desire to be in union with the love, beauty, truth, and happiness found in God. As Saint John Paul II also wrote, expressing much the same idea, all persons are called to greatness so that their souls desire to come into union with God who is love and whose love makes all things whole.

When the early Christians, and especially Augustine, encountered pagan philosophy and poetry they were moved by the beauty and the signs of truth that they saw. More recently, Christians like C.S. Lewis have noted that if Christians truly believe in a living God who is the creator of the cosmos then why is it not possible that this God dispensed signs of truth and beauty to the pagans in preparation for the eventual incarnation of Christ? The idea that all things beautiful and truthful (no matter their gradation away from the fullness of truth) are really signs pointing, and belonging, to God has long been a pillar to Christianity and Christian culture.

Christianity proclaims, through the doctrine of *imago Dei*, that all persons are made in love for love. Love, as the intention of union between two things, is a natural and instinctively social endeavor. *Harmonia*, after all, requires at least two partners to be in union together; one cannot be in harmony by itself but only with and through an other. Solitude, by definition, cannot be harmonious. Like Gallus, then, we who live in loneliness and shut ourselves off from love (failing to yield to love) suffer, though we may have, at some point in our lives, tasted the nectar of love that makes life sweet and calls us home. Tragic indeed. But within that tragedy are the seeds of truth.

In contrast to solitude and loneliness, human love and friendship, according to Augustine, allow us to participate in the love that defines the divine Trinity. Just as the Trinity is a "relations of love," so too is friendship between humans a relationship governed by love. The highest expression of this participation in love is love consummated through marriage. In reading Virgil, along with other classical authors, Augustine saw the traces of this truth in the yearning cries for friendship and love.

Friendship and marriage allow us to practice *imitatio Dei* (imitation of God, who is Love). When two (or more, in friendship) images of divine love are united together in harmony the participation of love which occurs becomes a mirror of the love of the Trinity. Augustine poetically summarized this reality as such, "When we see love, we see the Trinity."

This returns us to the great sage and poet who became a guide and father figure to Dante in hell and purgatory. Virgil is right that love is a real and powerful force in the world. He is right that it is a beautiful and desirable thing for people to seek union with one another in love. He is right that love is rational as well as instinctive. He is right that we should yield to love and that love conquers all things. Augustine may have wept for Dido because he was originally trapped in carnal love and beauty; but even carnal love and beauty are signs of the true love and beauty of God when properly understood and ordered, thereby directing one toward the upward union with Supreme Goodness as they "sing songs of ascent."

This is what the Church Fathers understood when they read Virgil. There was tremendous beauty in the writings and themes of the greatest of the Roman poets. One cannot help but be moved to tears when reading Virgil, just as Augustine was. (Even more-so in Latin where the lyrical grace of Virgil can be fully heard.)

Where Virgil went wrong, however, was to associate desire only with other humans, locating the hope of desiring fulfillment in another human rather than the source of transcendent love itself that makes humans beautiful. Virgil's humanism, therefore, is but a shadow to the humanism offered in Christian anthropology where the human soul and person finds greater fulfillment through love of God. Christianity's vision of love offers an even greater humanism than Virgil, for through the image of God in us, humans are made even more beautiful. In recognizing the divine image within us, Augustine would argue in *De Trinitate*, we are made all the more beautiful since beauty comes with understanding and not just pathos.

Nevertheless, Virgil's themes ring true to any Christian: signs pointing to the truth, love, and beauty that is God—this is what Augustine and the early Fathers understood in reading Virgil and why

Virgil's always had a longstanding place within the Christian literary canon though he himself was not a Christian. Virgil's themes, from Christian eyes, are signs pointing to the revelation of Christ and the Church. Here we find the enduring and eternal power of love and how it binds all things together and how only in this union through love the desires of the heart can be satisfied. Virgil was close, as close as one could get prior to the revelatory incarnation of Love itself in flesh and blood.

The desire to love and the desire to be in union with another, as Dante weaves into the structure of his Christian poem (for he is only alone at the beginning when he is lost), is the driving force of salvation. Humans desire love and God desires us to love. In Christianity the two desiring flames of *amore/eros* come together in union which is then superseded by *agape*: the compassion and tender mercy that emerges out of that desiring love that brings souls together.

Unsurprisingly, Christian readers of Virgil saw the same spirit in his poetry. We ourselves, as readers, coming into relationship with Virgil's characters often end up having pity and compassion toward them—perhaps the finest realization of how that desire for love produces *agape*.

T. S. Eliot remarked that the loss of the classics, Greek and Latin, would spell the demise of Christianity and, eventually, the whole of Western civilization built on the heart of love which breeds compassion (and it should be noted that compassion is impossible without that desiring love which precedes it). Per the ironies of history, it seems that Virgil is now far closer to the Christian truth than many of us in the modern world drowning in relativism, proclaiming love is just the stimulation of atoms, and enslaving ourselves to the tyranny of technology. But that also means that in reading Virgil—just as the Church Fathers did two millennia ago and Christians have done ever since—we may once again see the beauty and truth of the signs in Virgil's writings that can lead us back, and nearer, to Love itself. As Christians teaching and reading Virgil, we must never forget this.

So, on to your great honors, child! The time is near,
Dear child of the gods, great increment of Jove.
See how the vast round world bows down—
Land and tracts of seas and depthless skies.
See how all creation joys in the time to come!

May Beatrice indeed sing praises of Virgil to God. Virgil's writings capture the signs of the human spirit and condition. In the melancholic world of Antiquity Virgil stood out as a light in the darkness. But it was necessary to capture Virgil's signs of light and direct them to their source as the Church Fathers did. Perhaps the time is coming again when Virgil will be a bright light in the darkness and Christians will, once more, capture that light and orient the crying soul to the Good, True, and Beautiful rather than remain lovesick in bed or alone on golden sands. Our world cries out like Gallus for that healing love that mends the soul. Let us shepherd it to the only source of fulfilling love. Our souls depend on it.

DANTE IN THE DIGITAL INFERNO

T. S. Eliot famously said that "Dante and Shakespeare divide the world between them. There is no third." If people know Dante, it's probably related to his poem *The Divine Comedy*—specifically that part about hell. So people only read Dante for *The Inferno*, if they read him at all. Most, however, haven't read any part of his magisterial poem and probably have no intention to ever read him. But for those who have read him, or those who will read him, the question must inevitably be asked: Why did Dante have the pilgrimage through hell before ascending Mount Purgatory to take his seat in the choir of saints and angels to sing of "the Love that moves the sun and the other stars?"

In our digital age, Dante is once again journeying through hell. This time without Virgil as a guide or a literate audience knowing his references, allusions, and cultural inheritance. The inferno of social media has Dante wandering astray, lost, in the digital forest of ignorance and animosity.

For many people on social media, Dante is the often alluded to thirteenth century "Italian poet" who "invented" our modern understanding of hell. As one content creator put it, "the concept of hell as eternal conscious torment comes from a piece of Italian literature written in the 1300s and is no where in the Bible." This kind of ignorance proliferates digital space.

Admittedly, a lot of bad information about Dante and the belittling of his work comes as part of the larger theological and biblical wars waged in western culture that has spread online. As a former graduate student in religious studies and the Bible from Yale, it is rather heartbreaking to see the continuous promotion of misinformation online, especially since it is the misinformation that gets the most traction while a few heroic biblical scholars and professors—almost always on their own free time—take to social media to offer corrections.

On the issue of Dante inventing hell because it is nowhere found in the Bible, a very common retort by online activists with very little to no education in the formation of the Hebrew Bible and the Christian New Testament, the idea of hell as a place of eternal conscious torment is, in fact, found in Scripture. The conceptualization of hell as a place for the punishment of the wicked can be identified rather clearly in the Hellenistic period of late Hebrew Bible literature, Daniel and Trito-Isaiah are the most notable examples. Furthermore, late Second Temple period Judaism was a time of great theological and religious innovations; a lot of extrabiblical literature from the apocalyptic traditions in this period deal with hell and the soul after death. These extrabiblical traditions eventually influenced the New Testament, especially the Gospels, where Jesus very frequently speaks of hell, punishment, and the soul's torment after death. While this is well-known to biblical scholars and grad students, it remains ignored by a new wave of "digital creators" waging wars online for their own reasons—some sympathetic, others, not so much.

Dante, unfortunately, has become a casualty in this fight. As another social media content creator crudely put it, "Dante invented hell."

While Dante's imagination of hell in the *Divine Comedy* has been culturally influential, this belittling of Dante within wider conspiratorial disputes in digital space marginalizes the greatness of Dante and his epic poem. Since Dante didn't create hell, and since most people are probably only now receiving some knowledge of Dante secondhand through these online antics, why should we read Dante and, in particular, *The Inferno*? Far from delighting in the misery of the damned, Dante's *Inferno* is all about pity: pity for the damned, for it is in Dante's learning of pity which leads to a moment of forgiveness between he and Virgil which allows the poet pilgrim to escape the fires of hell and begin that ascent up the slopes of Mount Purgatory and enter into the blessed realm of the white rose where Love eternal abides. Dante's tears for the damned lead to his salvation.

"Midway along the journey of our life / I woke to find myself in a dark wood / for I had wandered off from the straight path." That is the famous opening of Dante's great epic of the human soul and its pilgrimage through hell to heaven. But we must ask ourselves, what exactly is hell to Dante and why must he first journey through the dark crevices of the city of Dis and the Malebolge before ascending Mount Purgatory to the abode of Eternal Love?

Dante is an exile, both in real life and in his spiritual life. However, the journey undertaken through *The Inferno* is more than that. It is a journey into the heart: the heart of misdirected love and, finally, the desecration of the intellect as the passions of violence overwhelm rationality to the point of people willfully rejecting Truth for the false lies of heresy and violence.

Some knowledge of the Christian theological tradition that informed Dante is necessary before we go on. Augustine, most famously, explained sin as misdirected love. In some sense, sin is not unnatural but the misapplication of an originally (and still naturally) good passion: the desire for love. Augustine also formulated the basic doctrine of the *imago Dei* that would guide western theology: to be made in the image of God meant to be made in love for love and in wisdom for wisdom. Unlike today's language where being made in the image of God is rhetorically used to imply human dignity and human rights (concepts alien to the patristic fathers), Augustine meant it as an interior reality: we can love and come to know love. In *De Trinitate*, Augustine would go as far as to assert that the prime image of God in man is the rational intellect.

Dante stands on Augustine's shoulders. The first circles of hell, properly speaking beginning with the circle of lust rather than Limbo, deal with misdirected love and mirror Augustine's infamous weeping statement in *Confessions* that he was "in love with the idea of love" but didn't know what love actually was. Beyond the River Styx when Dante and Virgil enter the city of Dis, the misdirected love that Dante encountered is now replaced by willful rejection of truth and nature. This is what heresy is. This rejection of truth and nature breeds lies and deceit, all the way to deception of nations, families, and friends (the ninth circle) culminating in betrayal and murder. Dante's roadmap through hell is a literary-theological imagining of the Augustinian understanding of man and sin.

While there is a sort of neat division between the two halves of hell, what is universal across Dante's journey is how he learns love, principally through pity which culminates in an act of forgiveness between he and Virgil, which permits his escape from hell. The message is clear: proper love guides us out of the inferno we have trapped ourselves in. In the circle of the lustful damned, Dante meets two illicit lovers. Francesca da Rimini and Paolo Malatesta carried on an affair for over a decade before it was discovered.

During Dante's conversation with Francesca, the reader learns that Francesca (and Paolo by extension) refuse to accept their own sin. They blame others. This is another recurring theme in hell. The damned refuse to acknowledge their own sin. Pride really does come before the fall. Their inability to acknowledge any wrongdoing and their willful blaming of others seals their fate. But it doesn't have to seal ours. Dante, the in-situ incarnation of the reader, tears up and takes pity on Francesca. Damned and damnable as she is, she still deserves our love. "Love your enemy," Christ declares in the Sermon on the Mount. Dante eventually faints in pity of the sad story that Francesca relates:

> "There is no greater pain
> than to remember in our present grief,
> past happiness (as well your teacher knows)!
>
> But if your great desire is to learn
> the very root of such a love as ours,
> I shall tell you, but in words of flowing tears.
>
> One day we read, to pass the time away,
> of Lancelot, of how he fell in love;
> we were alone, innocent of suspicion.
>
> Time and again our eyes were brought together
> by the book we read; our faces flushed and paled.
> To the moment of one line alone we yielded:
>
> it was when we read about those longed-for lips
> now being kissed by such a famous lover,
> that this one (who shall never leave my side)
>
> then kissed my mouth, and trembled as he did.
> Our Galehot was that book and he who wrote it.
> That day we read no further." And all the while
>
> the one of the two spirits spoke these words,
> the other wept, in such a way that pity
> blurred my senses; I swooned as though to die,
>
> and fell to Hell's floor as a body, dead, falls.

It's hard not to be Dante. Dante is us. Francesca and Paolo's story is tragic. But they made themselves their own idols. Still, Dante relates the pity he took. He did not delight in their misery. He did not mock them in their error. He wept with the damned. In doing so, he saved his own soul. Delight in another's misery, mockery and scorn afflicted onto others, is not the path to heaven. Love is. That is what Dante learns as he journeys through hell.

As Dante learns love through hell, his relationship with Virgil changes. Initially, when they first met, there was a lack of trust between the two. Yet this lack of trust is overcome with a compassion that grows between the two great poets. When Dante and Virgil approach the gates of the city of Dis, Virgil, terrified and taking compassion on the foolish Dante (Virgil has by now come to realize a certain spirit of foolishness governs Dante), he places his arm to shield the pilgrim-poet's eyes from Medusa:

> "Now turn your back and cover up your eyes,
> for if the Gorgon comes and you should see her,
> there would be no returning to the world!"
>
> These were my master's words. He turned me round
> And did not trust my hands to hide my eyes
> But placed his own on mine and kept them covered.

Although Virgil still doesn't trust Dante, he does have compassion toward him. He cares for Dante. And Dante begins to recognize, as these words indicate, that Virgil cares for him. This is the beginning of a relationship of love, compassion, mercy, and friendship that is otherwise devoid throughout all the levels of hell. The love that the two poets begin to form toward each other and share for each other is the means by which they will be able to leave the accursed abode of the loveless dead. Love literally does give new life is what Dante is telling us.

The culmination of love in hell is an act of forgiveness. Without forgiveness there is no reconciliatory bridge to a new life. Without forgiveness, there is no love. Forgiveness is the ultimate act of love for forgiveness is what permits love to unite as Saint Thomas Aquinas wrote, love is "the unitive force." Forgiveness is the essential heart of love which allows for reunification.

As Dante and Virgil are continuing through hell, Virgil carries Dante down the slopes of the Malebolge:

> Then he took hold of me with both his arms,
> And when he had me firm against his breast,
> He climbed back up the path he had come down.
>
> He did not tire of the weight clasped tight to him,
> But brought me to the top of the bridge's arch,
> The one that joins the fourth bank to the fifth.
>
> And here he gently set his burden down—
> Gently, for the ridge, so steep and rugged,
> Would have been hard even for goats to cross.
>
> From there another valley opened to me.

Here we see our two poet pilgrims literally united in helping each other. Yet Dante, aloof as he has been throughout the poem so far, is dilly dallying and this dilly dallying enrages Virgil who loses his temper:

I was listening, all absorbed in this debate,
when the master said to me: "Keep right on looking,
a little more, and I shall lose my patience."

I heard the note of anger in his voice
and turned to him; I was so full of shame
that it still haunts my memory today.

Like one asleep who dreams himself in trouble
and in his dream he wishes he were dreaming,
longing for that which is, as if it were not,

just so I found myself: unable to speak,
longing to beg for pardon and already
begging for pardon, not knowing that I did.

"Less shame than yours would wash away a fault
greater than yours has been," my master said,
"and so forget about it, do not be sad.

If ever again you should meet up with men
engaging in this kind of futile wrangling,
remember I am always at your side."

In this moment we see the forgiveness that Dante and Virgil exhibit to each other. Dante asks Virgil's forgiveness even without asking it with his voice—he seeks forgiveness with his face. Virgil recognizes this and bestows it. But he also recognizes his own errors and tells Dante "If ever again you should meet up with men / engaging in this kind of futile wrangling, / remember I am always at your side." After this remarkable moment, the moment that the entire pilgrimage of pity and love has been leading to, Dante and Virgil enter the final abode of hell where they eventually walk across the ice of treachery, see Satan eating the bodies of Judas, Brutus, and Cassius, then slip out of hell and begin their ascent to the stars, to heaven.

Dante's hell, contrary to the inaccurate, ignorant, and sometimes even deliberately deceitful representation of it on TikTok and across the broader abyss of digital space, isn't meant to terrify anyone. It is meant to instruct. Specifically, instruct in love. Dante calls on us to have pity and compassion for sinners. Pity and compassion for everyone. More importantly, the love that grows from pity and compassion must be realized in forgiveness. If we cannot love and cannot forgive then we really will entrap ourselves in hell, for hell is a loveless place created by the pride, passion, and deceit of the self which reign supreme at the expense of all others.

The Inferno is a deeply inspiring work within the *Divine Comedy*. It is, personally, my favorite of the three parts. Dante gives us a road-map, a guide, on how to flee from the Sodom and Gomorrah we have created for ourselves. Love is the remedy. Love is our hope. Love will save us. May we, with Dante, love those who misrepresent him and hope that they will come to learn the beauty of his message.

POWER, GLORY, AND VANITY: THE POLITICS OF ROMANTIC POETRY

"And on the pedestal these words appear: / 'My name is Ozymandias, king of kings: / Look on my works, ye Mighty, and despair!' / Nothing beside remains. Round the decay / Of that colossal wreck, boundless and bare / The lone and level sands stretch far away." Percy Bysshe Shelley's famous poem "Ozymandias" captures, in my opinion, the essence of the power, glory, and fleeting vanity of the political sentiments of the nineteenth century Romantics. While the Bible and classical sources testified to the vanity of fleeting power and glory, the Romantics resurrected this wisdom in an age of haughty power, glory, and egoism with a corresponding pomp, vanity, and egoism of their own which proves ironic, all things considered.

Understanding Romanticism is difficult because of the multifaceted avenues it influenced. Isaiah Berlin, in his series of lectures on Romanticism in 1964, remarked that Romanticism simultaneously influenced reactionary movements as much as radical and progressive movements. If, however, we are to agree upon one common thread of Romanticism it would have to be the unbridled passion, pathology, that undergirded it as it rebelled against the sterile and suffocating tyranny of mechanical materialism which had risen to prominence in the so-called Age of Enlightenment. Some have taken to calling the romantic revolution not so much the Counter Enlightenment as it was the Age of Passion.

The Age of Passion, to my mind, is apt. One cannot help but feel the passionate blood coursing through their own veins and off their lips as they read the words of proto-Romantics like Milton and Pope and the works of the canonical Romantics like Lord Byron, John Keats, or Shelley. And it is these three figures whom I would like to briefly discuss within the realm of the passionate politics of power, glory, and vanity which move their poems.

That the Romantics would preoccupy themselves with politics shouldn't be surprising to us. After all, they lived in an age of intense passion and conflagration. Byron, Keats, and Shelley all matured and lived in the throes of the French Revolution and the Napoleonic Wars. Napoleon, unsurprisingly, is a figure whose echoes can be heard in their poetry—explicitly or implicitly. From the storming of the Bastille up until the Battle of Waterloo, the explosive triumph of the will stirred the hearts and passions of men and women in Europe and even across the sea in America. It was also an age of exploration, excavation, and desecration; all these themes meet in Romantic poetry in their unique ways.

It would seem odd, then, that some Romantic political poetry draws on the imagery and consciousness of antiquity rather than nascent modernity. But Romantic poetry using the veil and imagery and language of antiquity is making commentary on the present. The haughty tyrants of Europe were, in the imagination of the Romantics, akin to the cruel and vindictive kings of the past: Nebuchadnezzar, Ozymandias (Ramses II), Sennacherib.

Keats, if I am permitted to say, is the least of the three poets insofar that his language conveys the point in an otherwise straightforward way. It lacks the imaginative flair of Byron and Shelley but still underscores the main point of pride cometh before the fall. And who can forget, among the Biblically literate, the pride and fall of Nebuchadnezzar from towering conqueror and tyrant to bestial animal roaming with the cattle:

Before he went to live with owls and bats,
Nebuchadnezzar had an ugly dream,
Worse than a housewife's, when she thinks her cream
Made a naumachia for mice and rats:
So scared, he sent for that "good kind of cats,"
Young Daniel, who did straightway pluck the beam
From out his eye, and said—"I do not deem
Your sceptre worth a straw, your cushions old door mats."
A horrid nightmare, similar somewhat,
Of late has haunted a most valiant crew
Of loggerheads and chapmen;—we are told
That any Daniel, though he be a sot,
Can make their lying lips turn pale of hue,
By drawing out—"Ye are that head of gold!"

Keats, here, no doubt wishes himself to be the imaginative radical Daniel of his fancy (part of the romantic imagination of the poet-prophet being more eternal and immortal than their political masters who are, in fact, puppets to the poets who are the true masters). Daniel, like the poet Keats himself—an opponent of absolutism—reminds the pride and pomp of Nebuchadnezzar, the metaphor for the European kings and aristocrats of his own time, that his "sceptre" is only "worth a straw" and his "cushions old door mats." As a poet Keats mocks the pride and power of the vain king. Keats is speaking through Daniel.

As Daniel, Keats is telling the unworthy kings of the world (Nebuchadnezzar) of their coming fall which horrifies them. Truly, this prophecy of coming demise is an "ugly dream"—a terrible nightmare. Here, Keats also relishes the fact that the poet is like the prophet, interpreting dreams and visions with intense political overtures still relevant in our time as it was in ancient times. Power, glory, wealth—all is vanity since it will come tumbling down.

The straightforwardness of Keats's political romanticism reaches fuller maturation in Byron and Shelley. There is a lack of life, no life-force, to Keats's ostentatiously political poems (which is opposite of the very animating lyrical eroticism of Keats's romance poems and unfortunate since it shows the talent that Keats had). Byron's political poetry which draws on ancient language, imagery, and metaphor—by contrast—explodes to life before collapsing into death by the greater power of the angel of death and the hand of God:

The Assyrian came down like the wolf on the fold,
And his cohorts were gleaming in purple and gold;
And the sheen of their spears was like stars on the sea,
When the blue wave rolls nightly on deep Galilee.

Like the leaves of the forest when Summer is green,
That host with their banners at sunset were seen:
Like the leaves of the forest when Autumn hath blown,
That host on the morrow lay withered and strown.

For the Angel of Death spread his wings on the blast,
And breathed in the face of the foe as he passed;
And the eyes of the sleepers waxed deadly and chill,
And their hearts but once heaved, and for ever grew still!

And there lay the steed with his nostril all wide,
But through it there rolled not the breath of his pride;
And the foam of his gasping lay white on the turf,
And cold as the spray of the rock-beating surf.

And there lay the rider distorted and pale,
With the dew on his brow, and the rust on his mail:

And the tents were all silent, the banners alone,
The lances unlifted, the trumpet unblown.

And the widows of Ashur are loud in their wail,
And the idols are broke in the temple of Baal;
And the might of the Gentile, unsmote by the sword,
Hath melted like snow in the glance of the Lord.

While Byron is undeniably playing on the same themes of haughty power and pride being culled by a pertinent justice as in Keats, Byron brings a grander flair to his writings as the poem literally moves with the imagery of wind, life, and movement before dissipating into defeat, death, and lack of movement. The poem opens with power and majesty—temporal, to be sure—on full display, a grandiose movement of power and life: "The Assyrian came down like the wolf on the fold, / And his cohorts were gleaming in purple and gold; / And the sheen of their spears was like stars on the sea, / When the blue wave rolls nightly on deep Galilee." The power and majesty of the powerful Assyrian king and army, however, rapidly dissolves into death, destruction, and defeat: "And there lay the rider distorted and pale, / With the dew on his brow, and the rust on his mail; / And the tents were all silent, the banners alone, / The lances unlifted, the trumpet unblown."

In a grand movement of poetic successions and contrasts, the mighty power of Assyria pales in comparison to the greater power and majesty of the Angel of Death sent by the Lord to deliver Jerusalem from destruction. The once rapturous and awesome sight of banners and men and spears glistening in the sun as they move down the hills and valleys is suddenly stalled into a lifeless death, everything now "unlifted" as the wind howls through the camp and flaps the empty tents with only the echoing of flapping fabric filling the ear.

The height of pride and power is shown to be vain, all power and glory—as Byron shows here—is fleeting. "And the widows of Ashur are loud in their wail, / And the idols are broke in the temple of Baal; / And the might of the Gentile, unsmote by the sword, / Hath melted like snow in the glance of the Lord." The power of Sennacherib and his mighty army is nothing compared to the power of the Lord on High. Lords and ladies of temporal polities beware, challenge the awesome power of Lord if you dare.

The arrogance of the kings of old and the vanity of their passion and pride is also set up for the chopping block by Shelley. Like Byron, Shelley's "Ozymandias" opens with action and movement but reminds us of age and antiquity (and therefore decadence and decrepitness). But unlike Byron, who crushes the arrogance of tyrannical kings with a lifeless camp lacking movement, Shelley keeps movement alive through the cycle of time and its bearing down and withering away of the vanity of kings:

> I met a traveller from an antique land,
> Who said—"Two vast and trunkless legs of stone
> Stand in the desert. Near them, on the sand,
> Half sunk a shattered visage lies, whose frown,
> And wrinkled lip, and sneer of cold command,
> Tell that its sculptor well those passions read
> Which yet survive, stamped on these lifeless things,
> The hand that mocked them, and the heart that fed;
> And on the pedestal, these words appear:
> My name is Ozymandias, King of Kings;
> Look on my Works, ye Mighty, and despair!
>
> Nothing beside remains. Round the decay
> Of that colossal Wreck, boundless and bare
> The lone and level sands stretch far away."

What Shelley does so remarkably in this poem, upon close examination, is how it begins with a sense of urgency, movement, and life; we meet a traveler from an antique land who bears supposed wisdom and knowledge to the poetic pilgrim. But we soon learn that the amazing colossus that the ancient traveler has seen is "shattered" and "lifeless." And to make it more haunting, the ultimate revelation of the decayed statue is laid bare to us only after the ultimate invocation of arrogance and pride on the part of the patron and benefactor: "My name is Ozymandias, King of Kings; / Look on my Works, ye Mighty, and despair!" Only after Ozymandias boasts like an infantile tyrant do we learn what remains of that "colossal Wreck."

The arrogance of Ozymandias moves the world into the imbalance of decay. Decadence and destruction follow from this decay wrought by tyrannical arrogance. Destruction, Shelley reminds us, naturally follows such haughty proclamations of naked vanity. Yet the movement of nature, the eternality of lifeless things, persists. Ozymandias is dead. But the lifeless stones which bear his legacy, decayed as they are, remain without him—mocked by the eternality of the poet as he laughs at the pretensions of a failed king. Additionally, the "lone and level sands stretch far away." Befitting Shelley's atheism in comparison to Byron's despairing and psychological Calvinism, the power of man is nothing compared to the power of nature.

But allegories and metaphors of contemporary politics veiled by the imagery and consciousness of antiquity is not the only commonality among the Romantics. Given that Keats, Byron, and Shelley lived during the turbulence and exhilaration of the French Revolutionary and Napoleonic Wars, it is only fitting that Napoleon, the Napoleonic Wars, and Europe's titanic struggle against a new Sennacherib or Ozymandias—even if the poets themselves had awkward affinities to the French emperor reflective, perhaps, of the first realization of the psychology of frenemies—appear in their poetic writings. Paradoxically, or contradictorily depending on your perspective on the Romantics, our poets eulogize the pride and power of Napoleon but, in doing so, end by reminding us of the fleeting nature of glory and the vanity of power.

Keats is the most modest of the poets writing about the shocking and sudden fall of Napoleon—in 1814—and the first hopeful sway of peace to arrive on the continent since 1792. Napoleon goes unnamed, but "On Peace" echoes with the footsteps of Napoleon everywhere:

> O Peace! and dost thou with thy presence bless
> The dwellings of this war-surrounded Isle;
> Soothing with placid brow our late distress,
> Making the triple kingdom brightly smile?
> Joyful I hail thy presence; and I hail
> The sweet companions that await on thee;
> Complete my joy let not my first wish fail,
> Let the sweet mountain nymph thy favourite be,
> With England's happiness proclaim Europa's Liberty.
> O Europe! let not sceptred tyrants see
> That thou must shelter in thy former state;
> Keep thy chains burst, and boldly say thou art free;
> Give thy kings law leave not uncurbed the great ;
> So with the horrors past thou'lt win thy happier fate!

While Keats is genuinely happy for the arrival of peace, "Joyful I hail thy presence; and I hail / The sweet companions that await on thee," he is also hopeful for a continuation of reformist radicalism to sweep the cornerstones of Old Europe, those "former state[s]," away. "Let not sceptred tyrants see / That thou must shelter in thy former state; / Keep thy chains burst, and boldly say thou art free; / Give they kings law leave not uncurbed the great; / So with the horrors past thou'lt win they happier fate!" Keats desires to see a Europe free of the absolutist chains which currently ensnare it. He desires constitutional systems where laws constrain "the great" and provide the "happier fate" of the citizenry.

In between the lines we still learn much about Keats in this sonnet. He wants the powerful and proud to be curtailed. He wants the common citizenry to burst out of the absolutist chains that drag them down. Though it has the veil of modesty and reform, Keats desires nothing less than the powerful and prideful to be knocked down off their pedestals. The emancipatory impulse is what drives this desire to the see the proud and powerful broken.

Byron and Shelley also join the fray of Napoleonic eulogies. What make Byron and Shelley unique, in this enterprise, is that there is an undercurrent of adoration to their poems that nonetheless end with that proverbial wisdom of all power and glory is fleeting.

Action, movement, is the great hallmark of power and greatness as Shelley subtly informs us in "To the Emperors of Russia and Austria" in his imaginative poetic lecture on the Battle of Austerlitz. The "Coward Chiefs" of Russia and Austria remain "calm and still" on the heights as the torrential bloodbath ensues below where real patriots fight and die. Napoleon, by contrast, is the man of action—the "restless fiend who haunts / The tumult of yon gory field, / Whom neither shame nor danger daunts, / Who dares not fear, who cannot yield, / Will not the Equalizing blow / Exalt the high, abase the low, / And in one mighty shock o'erthrow / The slaves that sceptres wield." Cowardly tyrants sit aloft while men of greatness get into the thick of it.

But on the death of Napoleon Shelley was overcome to offer his eulogy to the great shaker and world mover. While others mocked and punned the French emperor, Shelley took it upon himself to offer a stirring eulogy that is—nevertheless—still filled with irony given that grandeur and greatness and glory ends ignominiously.

Shelley combines his two great themes like in Ozymandias, the eternality and supremacy of nature over the greatness of man:

What! alive and so bold, O Earth?
Art thou not over-bold?
What! leapest thou forth as of old
In the light of thy morning mirth,
The last of the flock of the starry fold?
Ha! leapest thou forth as of old?
Are not the limbs still when the ghost is fled?
And canst thou more, Napoleon being dead?

How! is not thy quick heart cold?
What spark is alive on thy hearth?
How! is not his death-knell knolled?
And livest thou still, Mother Earth?
Thou wert warming thy fingers old
O'er the embers covered and cold
Of that most fiery spirit, when it fled—
What, Mother, do you laugh now he is dead?

Shelley displays his own passionate arrogance in conversing with Mother Earth who berates the poet, and Napoleon in the process:

"Who has known me of old," replied Earth,
"Or who has my story told?
It is thou who art over-bold."
And the lightening of scorn laughed forth
As she sung, "To my bosom I fold
All my sons when their knell is knolled,
And so with living motion all are fed,
And the quick spring like weeds out of the dead.

"Still alive and still bold," shouted Earth,
"I grow bolder, and still more bold.
The dead fill me ten thousandfold
Fuller of speed, and splendour, and mirth;
I was cloudy, and sullen, and cold,
Like a frozen chaos uprolled,
Till by the spirit of the mighty dead
My heart grew warm. I feed on whom I fed.

"I feed on whom I fed" is apt to describe this mortal condition of man and the empty grandeur and greatness that accompanies him. The Earth feeds on the poor and the rich, the haughty and the lame, the great and insignificant. It mattered not how great and powerful Napoleon was—like Ozymandias—Nature's power is tenfold that of man. So it is that Napoleon, the scourge of Europe—the bringer of liberty or tyranny depending your partisanship (and it is obvious where the sympathies of these English Romantics stood)—is swallowed up by the Earth and his grandeur and greatness but a ruin inside the stomach of that which consumes everything man has ever tried to achieve:

"Ay, alive and still bold," muttered Earth,
"Napoleon's fierce spirit rolled,
In terror, and blood, and gold,
A torrent of ruin to death from his birth.
Leave the millions who follow to mould
The metal before it is cold,
And weave into his shame, which like the dead
Shrouds me, the hopes that from his glory fled."

In fitting tribute, Shelley still gives Napoleon a "fierce" and rolling "spirit" to indicate his greatness, even if it is consumed by the Earth and all "glory [has] fled."

Byron's "Ode to Napoleon Buonaparte" is, in my mind, the grandest of the eulogistic (and satirical) compositions to the French Emperor concerned with his fall from power. Where Shelley has his own egotistical wrestling match with Nature and loses, Byron captures the blood, terror, and ecstasy of political greatness and decadence all at once. There is spectacle and ego, ecstasy and victory, glory and vanity, in this pursuit of power and eternity among great men. Yet there is also the reality that grandeur is soon met by the fall:

> 'Tis done—but yesterday a King!
> And arm'd with Kings to strive—
> And now thou art a nameless thing:
> So abject—yet alive...
>
> The triumph, the vanity,
> The rapture of the strife—
> The earthquake voice of Victory,
> To thee the breath of life;
> The sword, the sceptre, and that sway
> Which man seem'd made but to obey,
> Wherewith renown was rife—
> All quell'd!—Dark Spirit! What must be
> The madness of thy memory.

The opening stanzas of Bryon's poetry proceeds paradoxically. The great movement, power, and vanity of Napoleon has become the movement of memory in Byron. The poem begins with the death and destruction of Napoleon, now a "nameless thing." But upon reflecting on that former greatness, Byron provides the spectacle and ego, ecstasy and victory, the "rapture of the strife" which moves grandiosity to ascend to the stars.

In continuing to reflect upon Napoleon, we meet the awesome wrestling of power against power, the fragility of the old coming up against the youthful intemperance of the new, freedom for all and the destruction of the old. In this conflagration of old power and new power, youthful exuberance and aged fear, the intensity of the sublime is revealed in this struggle to the death:

> And Earth hath spilt her blood for him,
> Who thus can hoard his own!
> And Monarchs bow'd the trembling limb,
> And thank'd him for a throne!
> Fair Freedom! we may hold thee dear,
> When thus thy mightiest foes their fear
> In humblest guise have shown.
> Oh! ne'er may tyrant leave behind
> A brighter name to lure mankind!
>
> Thine evil deeds are writ in gore,
> Nor written thus in vain—
> Thy triumphs tell of fame no more,
> Or deepen every stain:
> If thou hadst died as died as honour dies,
> Some new Napoleon might arise,
> To shame the world again—
> But who would soar the solar heights,
> To set in such a starless night?

What Byron does well in his eulogy concerning the fall of Napoleon is how greatness lives on in memory even as battlefield triumphs and magnificent marble statues are no more. Great men come and go, their monuments decay and dissolve, but in that most blessed realm of memory greatness endures in the imagination of the beholder. Yet that memory reminds us of fleeting vanity, that no matter how great and powerful one was, death and destruction inevitably come.

Power, Glory, and Vanity all intersect in the mesmerizing movement of Romantic poetry. The rapturous strife that was the 1790s-1810s is captured in the very movement and closure of the political poetry of the Romantics. We witness power, pride, and glory—but we also witness death, destruction, and the fleeting and feeble realities of power and pride. All decays. All withers. All disappears. The Romantics, in their own egotistical ways, remind us of the ancient wisdom from antique lands that "all is vanity." From them we remember the decayed and desiccated ruins of fleeting politics, kings, queens, and tyrants.

The Romantics, as new preachers, still proclaim that timeless truth. But they do so with such a pomp and pride of their own that one wonders if they imbued into their proclamations a type of energetic motion that was intended to outlast their own vain lives that they knew would decay and die. And vain the lives of Keats, Shelley, and Byron were despite the beauty and truth contained in their poetry. They too reached pinnacles only to fall ignominiously, each and every one just like Sennacherib, Nebuchadnezzar, Ozymandias, and Napoleon.

NOTE

The Preface was originally published in *Crisis Magazine* under the title "A Catholic View of Poetry." The poem "As the Leaves Begin to Change" was originally published in *Merion West*, and the poems "Dance of the Sky" and "Where the Nereids Swim and Play" were originally published in *VoegelinView*. The essay "Virgil and the Christian Imagination" was originally published in *Front Porch Republic*. The essays "Dante in the Digital Inferno" and "Power, Glory, and Vanity: The Politics of Romantic Poetry" were originally published in *VoegelinView*. All previously published content have been republished in this book with permission from the editors. All other poems and the essay "Homer's Epic of Love" are original to this book. The quotations from Homer's *Iliad* and Dante's *Divine Comedy* come from the translations by Robert Fagles and Mark Musa respectively for the curious and gentle reader.

ABOUT THE AUTHOR

Paul Krause is a teacher, writer, and the editor-in-chief of VoegelinView. He is a frequent writer on the arts, classics, literature, music, politics, philosophy, and religion for numerous newspapers, magazines, and journals. His other books include *Muses on a Fire: Essays on Faith, Film, and Literature*; *The Odyssey of Love: A Christian Guide to the Great Books*; and *Finding Arcadia: Wisdom, Truth, and Love in the Classics*. Apart from teaching and writing, he is an avid hiker and those experiences often influence his creative writing and poetry.